Finches

by Stan Tekiela

Adventure Publications, Inc.
Cambridge, MN

Dedication

To my father, who loved Purple Finches.

Acknowledgments

Thanks to the Bird Collection, Bell Museum of Natural History, University of Minnesota (St. Paul) and the All Seasons Wild Bird Stores in Minnesota, which have been instrumental in obtaining the seed images in this book.

Thanks also to Jim and Carol Zipp, good friends and wild bird store owners, for reviewing this book.

Credits

Cover photos of birds by Stan Tekiela

All photos by Stan Tekiela except pg. 8 (Cassin's) by Brian E. Small; pg. 27 (bottom inset) from Shutterstock. All full-page bird images (except pg. 20) and the images on pg. 6 are American Goldfinches.

Edited by Sandy Livoti

Cover and book design by Jonathan Norberg

10 9 8 7 6 5 4 3 2 1

Copyright 2015 by Stan Tekiela
Published by Adventure Publications, Inc.
820 Cleveland Street South
Cambridge, MN 55008
1-800-678-7006
www.adventurepublications.net
All rights reserved
Printed in China
ISBN: 978-1-59193-530-8

Table of Contents

All About Finches

The American Goldfinch is one of our favorite backyard birds. Who doesn't enjoy the bold yellow plumage and black forehead of the males? Their musical songs and high-pitched calls bring our gardens to life. Flying in flocks, they are easy to attract to our feeders, making them some of our most desirable backyard birds.

Also known as Wild Canary, the American Goldfinch (*Carduelis tristis*) only superficially looks like a canary. It is a passerine, or perching bird, in Fringillidae, which is the Finch family. A petite bird with a short bill, notched tail and short pointed wings, the American Goldfinch is one of many finch species in North America. It is closely related to Pine Siskins, Lesser and Lawrence's Goldfinches, Common and Hoary Redpolls and others.

Unique among the finches, American Goldfinch males undergo dramatic seasonal color changes. During spring and summer they are bright yellow with black foreheads, but come winter they change their old feathers (molt) to new shades of olive yellow to olive green, appearing like the females. Females also molt, but their color changes are hardly noticeable.

American Goldfinches are unique in other ways as well. They are known for their distinctive songs, undulating flights, and their nearly exclusive diet of seeds. They are gregarious all year but nest later in the season. Unlike most birds, they don't migrate in predictable patterns.

male

female

Facts

Relative Size: the American Goldfinch is the same size as most warblers, wrens and sparrows

Length: 5" (13 cm)

Wingspan: 9–10" (23–25 cm)

Weight: .4–.5 oz. (11–14 g)

Male: bright yellow with a black forehead, small yellow-to-orange bill, black wings with a single white wing bar, notched black tail

Female: dull yellow with a brighter yellow chest, small yellow-to-pink bill, black wings and tail, lacks a black forehead

Juvenile: same as female

Nest: cup; 3–4" (7.5–10 cm) in diameter, 2–2.5" (5–6 cm) high; female constructs with plant materials, uses spiderwebs and caterpillar silk to hold it together

Migration: unpredictable, depends on the weather and availability of food; flocks of 20 or so birds move only far enough to find food

Food: mainly seeds and a small amount of insects, visits seed feeders; favors Nyjer seeds, also enjoys black oil sunflower seeds and hulled sunflowers

American Goldfinch

Purple Finch

House Finch

Pine Siskin

Common Redpoll

Hoary Redpoll

Red Crossbill

White-winged Crossbill

Evening Grosbeak

Pine Grosbeak

Lesser Goldfinch

Lawrence's Goldfinch

Gray-crowned Rosy-Finch

Cassin's Finch

Range & Habitat

The range of the American Goldfinch is widespread, spanning the Lower 48 and reaching into Canada and down into Mexico. Studies of banded goldfinches show that many don't have regular or predictable migratory patterns. Instead, they wander around the country, usually in small flocks, with females moving farther than the males. The transient movement seems to be tied to food sources in open fields, scrubby places and woodlands more than the seasons. Northern populations tend to travel much more than those in the South, and some southern populations don't move around at all.

Studies show that American Goldfinches banded in Ontario, Canada, were found later in Louisiana—more than 1,000 miles away! Flocks search for reliable food sources, traveling upwards of 5 miles each day.

Most other species of finches respond to changing food sources. For example, Common Redpolls, Pine Siskins, Pine Grosbeaks and White-winged Crossbills fly out of Alaska and Canada in winters when seed supplies are low. These birds are common in some areas in some years and scarce in others.

All finches move in flocks of the same species, but they are also well known for traveling in mixed flocks during winter. Flocks range from just a handful of birds to a couple dozen in summer to hundreds of birds in winter.

Maps represent most finch species in the United States and Canada.

■ Year-round　■ Summer　■ Winter

Songs & Calls

American Goldfinches are not only fun to watch, but they also sing wonderful songs. Their vocalizations consist of both songs and calls. Only male goldfinches sing, and only during summer. Often they create unique songs by repeating a phrase in rambling order.

Known for singing during courtship displays, a male goldfinch will fly in widely arching circles, flapping his wings and singing before gliding. It's as if he is on a roller coaster, flapping and singing while going up and silent when coasting down. You can see these displays above scrubby fields or open lots during summer.

You can often hear American Goldfinches sing on warm summer days with clear skies. Young goldfinch males learn the songs by listening to the adult males.

Finches give calls to communicate with each other daily. Goldfinches have five kinds of calls: contact, threat, alarm, distress and feeding calls.

QUICK-TIPS

- American Goldfinch songs sound like "po-ta-to-chip"
- Males sing only during the breeding season to defend their territory and attract a mate; females don't sing
- Songs are musical, long-lasting and highly variable with many notes and phrases
- To impress the females, male goldfinches sing from the treetops in their territory and during courtship flights
- Calls are non-musical, often harsh-sounding notes

Nests

American Goldfinches often build their cup nests in a fork of twigs or in the end (terminal) cluster of branches in small saplings or short evergreen trees. Sometimes they nest in shrubs, but they always need adequate space for the female to sit comfortably while incubating.

The female goldfinch will return to the immediate area where she hatched as a chick and choose a nest site. Her mate watches as she tries out several spots before beginning nest construction. She builds the nest entirely by herself. The male might contribute bits of material occasionally, but he spends most of his time watching for danger and for trespassing finches that may have the bravado to breed with the female while she builds.

Goldfinch nests are usually constructed 3–7 feet above the ground. The nests are so well built that they often hold water and can last for over a year!

It's not necessary to put out extra building materials for the female. She builds in three stages. First, she firmly attaches the base to twigs with spiderwebs. Next, she weaves the cup with a wide variety of plant fibers. Last, she lines the cup with soft thistledown or down from dandelion, goatsbeard and other plants. It's thought that the availability of plant down might be the reason why goldfinches wait so long in the season to nest.

Often the nest is camouflaged with lichen bits and other plant materials to help conceal it. Construction takes 4–10 days, and most are ready in an average of 6 days.

Eggs, Chicks & Juveniles

American Goldfinches are late-summer nesters and can therefore raise only 1–2 broods each season. In the southern states, they can have one more brood than in the cooler northern states, where winter starts earlier and there's less time to produce a second brood. Most start nesting in July and August, well after many other finches are done nesting. Chicks hatch days apart in the order of eggs laid (asynchronously). Naked and helpless, they can't control their body temperature, so the mother needs to sit on them (brood) until they grow enough feathers to keep warm. While the female broods, the male brings most of the food for his family.

Within just 11–15 days of hatching, the chicks leave the nest (fledge). At this time they are juveniles, nearly full size and look like their mother. They follow the parents, begging with open beaks, fluttering their wings and squawking loudly. Adults land close-by to feed them.

Broods: 1–2 per season

Clutch Size: 3–7 eggs (4–6 average)

Egg Length: .6" (1.5 cm)

Egg Color: pale blue or bluish white with no markings

Incubation: 10–12 days; female incubates

Hatchlings: naked except for sparse tufts of down feathers, with eyes and ears sealed shut

Fledging: 11–15 days

Finch Trivia

- The American Goldfinch is the official state bird of Iowa, New Jersey and Washington.

- Three goldfinch species occur in the United States: American, Lesser and Lawrence's Goldfinches.

- The genus name *Carduelis*, originating from *carduus*, the Latin word for "thistle," was given because goldfinches eat huge amounts of thistle seed and line their nests with the soft thistledown.

- Nyjer seed was formerly sold as Nyjer Thistle, but the name was a misnomer and misleading since Nyjer doesn't come from thistles. Now referred to as Nyjer seed or just Nyjer to avoid the weedy association.

- American Goldfinches, Pine Siskins and Common Redpolls are some of the few birds that can hang upside down to feed.

- Unlike chickadees, bluebirds and other songbirds, American Goldfinches don't eat many insects.

- Most American Goldfinches live about 3–5 years. The oldest, tracked through banding, lived nearly 11 years in the wild. In captivity they can live up to 10–12 years.

- Goldfinch males obtain their bold yellow coloration from carotenoid pigments in the food they consume. The more they eat, the brighter yellow the feathers.

- One of the few bird species that molts all of its body feathers twice a year; most other birds molt annually.

17

- The colors of the legs, feet and bill change with the season, just like the feathers. Lightly colored during the breeding season, these turn darker in winter.

- Timing of breeding, sexual selection and diet may all play a role in the color changes of male goldfinches.

- Females are more aggressive toward males during the summer; males are more dominant in winter.

- A male American Goldfinch defends a small territory of just one acre during the breeding season.

- The male American Goldfinch strengthens the pair bond with his mate by feeding her during courtship (allofeeding). The female postures like a juvenile finch and accepts the offering of food.

- The male goldfinch feeds the female when she is incubating the eggs.

- Most American Goldfinches nest only once during a breeding season. Older, more experienced females nest several weeks before the less experienced females and mate with a second male for a second brood in the same season when time permits.

- Often a host for Brown-headed Cowbird eggs. Many cowbird chicks expire within days, however, because the goldfinches regurgitate seeds to feed them and not insects that the cowbird babies require.

- American Goldfinches visit feeders during winter in large mixed flocks with Pine Siskins, Purple Finches and Common Redpolls.

- Evening Grosbeaks were mistakenly named because it was thought that they sang only in the evening.

- Purple Finch males are not actually purple but rather a rich raspberry red color.

- Both White-winged and Red Crossbills are named for their peculiar scissor-like bills. The tip of the top bill crosses over the lower bill and helps them extract seeds from cones.

White-winged Crossbill

Pine Siskins and
House Finch

Feeding Finches

Attracting American Goldfinches and other finches is fairly easy. With a simple combination of food, water and shelter, they will visit your feeding station. Finches are songbirds that feed mainly on seeds. They are not like other songbirds, which eat large amounts of insects or fruit, depending on the season. During winter they move around in search of abundant supplies of seeds from thistle, sunflowers, teasels and other weedy plants. This is the time that they visit backyard feeding stations offering Nyjer and sunflower seeds. In the summer other seeds are more plentiful, and they get much of their nutritional requirements met from the wild sources.

All finch species, specifically Pine Siskins and Common Redpolls, gather and feed in small to very large flocks. These gather in small flocks of fewer than 10 individuals during the breeding season. During the non-breeding season they group in flocks of several hundred. Some winters will bring these hundreds of birds to our feeders.

When finches are away from feeders, the flock flies around, searching for food. Birds at the front of the flock are the first to spot seeds. They land on the ground or on weedy plants and settle down to eat. The finches that are still flying sail over the feeding birds, landing slightly ahead, and begin to feed. This leapfrog pattern recurs when the finches from behind fly over the finches ahead and start to feed in front once again. This activity continues as long as the flock is ground feeding.

Feeding in large flocks has a number of advantages. When a flock moves around, all the finches are looking to find food supplies. If a single finch spies some dried seed heads, one call note will bring the entire flock to the position. In addition, all finches in the flock are watching for predators. Once danger is seen, an alarm call is given and the finches take flight. Finches wheeling around in the air can confuse an avian predator, such as a Cooper's Hawk. This behavior greatly increases the survival of an individual finch.

All finches spend a lot of time ground feeding in the wild. So putting out ground feeders or just scattering seeds on the ground is a great way to attract them. Once they come visiting, they will all fly to your tube feeders. The trick is to offer enough perches to accommodate the large winter flocks. Many people put out more finch feeders in winter and remove them in the summer months when the flocks are smaller.

American Goldfinches and other finches don't just feed on the ground in the wild. They are excellent at clinging to seed heads of all sizes and extracting the ripe seeds within. Seed heads are smaller and more lightweight than finches, so the birds can cling to even the weakest stem or branch. They hover around a desired plant and once they land, they hold on tightly and hang upside down when needed. Their acrobatic ways enable them to reach just about any seed. When a stem is so weak that it bends under the finch's weight, the bird simply rides the stem to the ground, where it feeds.

Finches have small bodies and strong feet, so just about any feeder with many perches will work. There are feeders with holes on the bottom of the perches to make sure that only finches can cling to them and get the feed. Providing a variety of tube feeders around 6–10 feet off the ground gives finches a number of food choices. See pages 35–37 to learn more about the types of feeders to use for finches.

Finches have unique conical-shaped bills. The edges of the upper bill have a groove that runs down each side. Once the jaw closes, the edge of the lower bill fits into this groove. When a finch opens a larger seed, such as a black oiler, it uses its tongue to maneuver the seed onto its edge between the upper and lower bill. The lower jaw moves up and splits the seed. At the same time the tongue helps to move the seed and peel the husk, exposing the kernel. The husks fall to the ground, and the finch eats the prize—just the edible remains.

Because they feed mainly on seeds and not insects, a water source is very important for all finch species. This can range from a plain birdbath to a complex waterfall. A shallow depth of 1 inch works best since finches must stand to bathe or drink without submerging. They bathe and drink often, perhaps more than other birds.

Small trees and tall shrubs near feeders provide safe living essentials and shelter. Shrubs and trees serve as staging areas where finches can check for danger before flying to feeders and birdbaths.

Seeds & Grains

Nyjer: Nyjer is a very tiny black seed that is cultivated from an African plant in the sunflower family. Grown in Africa, India and parts of Asia, Nyjer (*Guizotia abyssinica*) is sterilized to prevent it from sprouting and growing before being imported into the United States. Sterilization also protects our environment by killing any invasive weed seeds that may be imported with the Nyjer seed. Because of the extra expenses of heat treatment and overseas transportation, the cost of this seed is very high and has led to its other name, Black Gold.

Relatively new to the bird feeding industry, Nyjer seed has been used for only around 40–50 years. It's the favorite of many finch species, including the American Goldfinch, House Finch, Common Redpoll and Pine Siskin. It is a high-energy food that contains 35% fat, 18% protein and 18% fiber and is a popular feed to offer during winter due to its calorie content and fat.

Nyjer requires specialized feeders with tiny openings. The inedible hulls dropped from feeders will eventually cover and kill the grass or garden plants beneath if they are not blown or raked out.

Hulled Sunflower: Hulled sunflower is just the meat or nutmeat part of the sunflower seed without the inedible, hard outer shell. Because finches don't have to open the seed, this is a highly desirable food for them. The nutritional content is the same as black oil and striped sunflower seeds. There's no possibility for these seed hearts to germinate, so the bags are sold as non-germinating or no-mess mixes. With hulled sunflower, you don't need to rake up or blow away dropped hulls under feeders.

Hulled sunflower is often available as whole nuts or pieces or chips. The expense of shelling the seeds makes this feed more expensive than others, but the benefits may outweigh the cost. After all, most birdseed is sold by weight, and with hulled sunflower you are not paying for inedible shells.

Black Oil Sunflower: Black oil seeds are smooth black seeds that come from the common sunflower, *Helianthus annuus*. All finch species enjoy black oilers. They have little trouble cracking them open with their thin, narrow bills, and they spend a lot of time eating them.

Black oil seeds contain more fat from oil than other seeds, hence the name. They are meatier and more nourishing per bite than nearly any other bird food sold. Each seed has 28% fat, 15% protein and 25% fiber, and supplies vitamins B and E, calcium, iron and potassium.

White Millet: Millet is a soft-shelled, small round grain that comes from the millet plant, *Panicum milieaceum*. There are red, golden and striped varieties, but the most common for birds is proso millet, which is white.

White millet is a highly favored seed of all finches and has good nutritional content: 4% fat, 12% protein, 8% fiber, vitamin B and calcium. It's an affordable seed that is often offered in ground and tray feeders, but finches will also readily eat it from a standard tube feeder.

Striped Sunflower: Striped sunflower seeds have a thin white stripe. They are larger than black oilers, and they have a thicker hull, making them harder to split for most finch species. Nevertheless, finches do open them and enjoy them immensely. Occasionally called stripers, these are the sunflower seeds that people eat. High in fat, protein, fiber and vitamins, they are usually a part of any popular birdseed mix.

Milo or Sorghum: Milo, also called sorghum, is a fine food to offer finches, especially in the West. They enjoy this seed, so put it in a tray on the ground or directly on the ground. Seed blocks contain mostly milo. These last a long time and feed many birds.

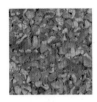

Cracked Corn: At an appealing low cost, cracked corn is a great option to feed large numbers of finches on the ground. It also draws rabbits, squirrels, raccoons, opossums, and other birds. Offerings of cracked corn will keep the squirrels busy with something to eat, leaving your bird feeders with the pricier foods for the finches alone.

Cracked corn is exactly what it sounds like—dried whole corn kernels that have been cracked. There can be a lot of dust associated with cracked corn, but it's worth it. This food won't sprout and grow in your garden or lawn, and finches eat the pieces whole, so there's no waste. Low in fat but high in protein and fiber, it is often a base in bird food blends. Offer it in large open-tray, fly-through or ground feeders or sprinkle it directly on the ground.

Grit: Not a seed, grit is composed of small granules of sand or tiny particles of rock and minerals. Commercial grit contains salt, an essential mineral that all finches need. Grit is stored in the gizzard. All bird species have a gizzard—a muscular stomach that crushes the larger pieces of seed that were swallowed. Birds lack teeth to grind their food, so the gizzard does the mashing. You can buy grit and add it to your tube and tray feeders that are sprinkled with mixed seeds. Finches also eat grit naturally on roadsides and in open fields.

Mixes

Finch Mix: Nearly every major retailer has its own version of a finch mix. It is a combination of Nyjer seed and finely chipped black oil sunflower seed hearts. The proportion of these two seed types varies from store to store, but usually it's about 50/50. This is the best mix for a wide variety of finch species. Offer it in a specialized feeder with tiny holes, and the finches will line up to take turns feeding.

Non-germinating Mix: Non-germinating mixes are composed of seeds that have been removed from their shells. These blends are excellent choices for finches because their small bills are not strong enough to easily split hulls open. Because seeds without shells will not germinate, people who do not want rogue sunflowers growing in their gardens or lawns may want to try these mixes.

Usually there are two varieties of seeds in these mixes: fine and coarsely ground sunflower hearts. These are extremely popular with all finches. Non-germinating may also contain whole nuts or chipped pieces of peanuts and other nuts, which finches may also eat. These mixes may look like the most expensive food per pound, but you're not paying for the hulls, which are included in the weight of other seeds but aren't eaten.

Premium or Deluxe Blend: Premium blends are often a base of black oil sunflower seeds with striped sunflower seeds and safflower. The addition of peanuts, shelled or whole, upgrades a regular blend to premium or deluxe. Sometimes mixes also contain raisins, cranberries or other dried fruit. Finches enjoy the sunflower offerings in this food. Great for winter, offer premium mixes when you want to offer special treats to attract finches and other species.

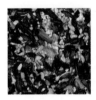

Specialty Mix: Many seed stores make a specialty blend that is unique to their store and works well for their region. In eastern states, black oil sunflower seed is the main ingredient. Western states often offer mixes with a heavy portion of milo. Stores may also mix in more peanuts or cracked or whole corn with the seeds. Finches visiting your feeders will readily pick through the specialty mix and eat their favorite seeds.

Storing Birdseed

Storing birdseed safely is easy. Keep it out of the house, preferably in a cool, dry place away from direct sunlight. Garages and sheds are the best places to stow feed since the cooler temperatures there will reduce the number of grain moths hatching out of seeds.

Transfer seed out of its original plastic or paper bag into a clean container. The container should be upright, semi-airtight and prevent mice, chipmunks and other rodents from chewing through and getting to the seed. Metal garbage cans are good choices for storage. Use several to store different kinds of food.

Try to avoid buying bird food in very large quantities. Pick up just enough to feed finches for a month or so. Make sure you use up the oldest seed before opening your more recent purchases.

Nyjer gets stale quickly due to the heat sterilization and long transport. If you aren't going through it quickly, it's best not to pick up large amounts. Also, purchase Nyjer from stores that sell a lot of it so you're getting only the freshest of seeds.

Feeding Q&A

Why do finches like Nyjer seed so much?

Nyjer seeds are very similar in size and nutrition to the wild seeds that most finches eat. Nyjer seed is soft, and finches split it open easily with their small bills.

Black oil and striped sunflower seeds—what's the difference?

Black oil sunflower seeds have around 70 percent nutmeat compared with just 57 percent in striped seeds. They also provide more calories than striped seeds in the form of fatty oils.

Should I feed finches during summer?

The best time to feed and enjoy American Goldfinches is perhaps in the summer. The males are flashing their bright yellow breeding plumage and are a pleasure to watch. You can also hear their delightful musical song, which they don't sing during the non-breeding season.

If a lot of finches are visiting my feeders in winter, should I put up more feeders?

Responding to changing feeding habits is the key to attracting and enjoying the finches in your yard even more. When you notice more finches showing up during winter, it's always good to put up more Nyjer feeders to accommodate the extra visitors.

What if I leave town or take a vacation?

It's not true that when you start feeding finches, you can't stop. Finches do not become dependent on our feeders. They take advantage of the quick and easy offerings, but once those are gone they just fly off to another feeder or a wild food source. When you get back home, simply fill your feeders and watch the finches return. It won't take long.

What if I see a finch with a swollen eye?

A swollen eye on any finch means it has contracted the bacteria *Mycoplasma gallisepticum*, which causes avian conjunctivitis. A common disease in domestic turkeys and chickens, it is a respiratory disease that is spread among birds in close contact with each other at feeding stations. It's not always fatal, but many birds die from exposure or the inability to find food or avoid predators rather than from the disease itself.

What should I do with old seeds?

Birdseed can go bad over time. If seeds smell bad, the oils have gone rancid and the batch needs to be thrown out. Grain moths, spiders and other pests can infest old birdseed. While bugs won't affect the overall seed, they may be trouble in the house. Wet seeds will spoil and stick together. The resulting mold or mildew can be fatal to finches, so discard seeds at the first sign of decay. Sprouted seeds are also red flags for disposal. Rodent infestation means urine or feces in the seed and you should not use it.

Bird Feeders

Offering the right foods is certain to attract American Goldfinches, Pine Siskins and Common Redpolls and keep them coming back. All of these finches come to feeders that offer Nyjer seeds or chipped sunflower seeds. These are their primary sources of food.

Feeders with a tight mesh screen permit finches to cling to the sides while eating Nyjer seeds. The best styles use metal mesh. These do well in any weather and keep squirrels and larger birds from extracting the seeds.

Tube feeders with short perches allow finches to feed in comfort. If many finches visit, use one with more ports.

Finches are flock feeders, so put out a large tray feeder for flocks. American Goldfinches and all other finches in the wild feed on the ground. Scatter seeds around the area to attract them to your ground feeder.

QUICK-TIPS

- Use specialized Nyjer feeders when offering Nyjer seed
- Some of the best feeders for finches are tube feeders with small perches, which help deter larger birds
- Put larger seeds, such as black oil sunflower seeds, in your tray feeders
- When elevating tray feeders, use a squirrel baffle to keep unwanted critters from reaching the food
- Spread millet or other inexpensive food in a tray feeder 12 inches high and set it down for ground feeding

Feeder Types

Nyjer Feeder: Usually a long tube-shaped feeder constructed of fabric, metal mesh or plastic tubing. Tiny holes allow the slow release of the tiny seeds. Sock-like cloth bags are also popular Nyjer feeders.

Tube Feeder: A clear plastic tube with metal openings for accessing seeds, and pegs for perching. Small to large sizes hold different amounts of seeds. Some varieties have a bottom tray for spilled or extra seeds, which finches use as a landing platform and for perching. Hangs from a shepherd's hook or sets on top of a post or pole.

Platform, Tray or Ground Feeder: Also called a fly-through feeder. Usually has a flat, open surface for seeds. Hangs from a series of wires or chains, rests on a central post or pole, or sits on the ground with the bottom of the tray around 12 inches off the ground. Made of wood or metal and often has a series of holes or slots for drainage. Some have a protective roof.

Window Feeder: Made of lightweight plastic or wood. Suction cups adhere the feeders to windows for close-up viewing. See the Food & Feeder Quick-Chart on pages 40–41 for all the good finch foods you can use in these feeders.

Placing Feeders

Feeding finches is fun and easy, so put feeders where you can easily enjoy them. They should be in areas near your home where you spend a lot of time and in places where you can see outside clearly and comfortably.

Most feeding stations are about 20–40 feet away from residences. Placing feeders closer draws a wide variety of finches to where you can see them more easily. The closer the feeders, however, the more likely you will have window strikes.

Feeders close to shrubs or other cover give finches a place to stage and look for predators before flying in to feed. Plant cover also gives them a quick place to hide in case a hawk swoops in. Feeders in the middle of large open spaces work well for large flocks of finches. The flock often flies around and around the feeders before all the birds land together.

Place feeders where squirrels can't get to them. The basic placement rule is 5 feet and 8 feet—meaning feeders should be at least 5 feet off the ground and at least 8 feet from any other surface from which a squirrel can jump. This includes trees, houses, sheds, outdoor grills, birdbaths, patio furniture and anything else a squirrel can climb to jump onto feeders.

When placing feeders, be sure to install a squirrel or raccoon baffle on each one. Baffles are metal tubes that prevent these animals from climbing your shepherd's hooks and accessing the bird food.

Remember to do some ground feeding. This style of feeding attracts many finch species, so you'll want to scatter seed around your feeding station, but not in your flower garden. The constant scratching by the birds and the mat of hulls that accumulates will kill any plants you are trying to grow.

Choose a place where seed waste won't kill the grass. Perhaps landscape an area of the yard dedicated to bird feeding with rocks, shrubs and a water element.

Multiple feeders bring in larger numbers of finches. In fact, the more tube and Nyjer feeders you have, the more finches you will attract.

Food & Feeder Quick-Chart

Finches are food specialists mostly enjoying Nyjer seed. They also eat other foods. This chart lists their favorite foods and pairs them with the feeders.

FOOD	FEEDER TYPE Nyjer	Tube	Platform, Tray or Ground	Window
Nyjer	●	x	x	x
Finch Mix	x	●	○	○
Hulled Sunflower	x	●	○	○
Non-germinating Mix	x	●	○	○
Black Oil Sunflower	x	●	○	○
Premium or Deluxe Blend	x	●	○	○
White Millet	x	●	○	○
Specialty Mix	x	●	○	○
Striped Sunflower	x	●	●	○
Milo or Sorghum	x	○	○	○
Cracked Corn	x	x	○	x
Grit	x	○	○	○

● Best   ○ Good   ○ Acceptable

Maintaining Feeders & Good Practices

Feeder maintenance is vital for the overall health of all finches. How often you clean your feeders depends on the weather and season. Cleaning is more important in summer than winter, and feeders in wet environments need more cleaning than those in dry climes. Feeders offering food with a high oil content must be cleaned more often than those holding less fatty foods.

Bird feeders are the number one place where disease is spread. Dirty feeders hold bacteria, viruses and mold that can sicken or kill birds. If you see any finch with swollen or red eyes, stop feeding and clean your feeders. There is no proof that feeders spread the eye disease, but it won't hurt to be cautious and cleanly.

A number of transmissible diseases are associated with birds, including finches, and their droppings. To be safe, use good hygiene practices and take some basic precautions when filling or cleaning your feeders.

For example, when you clean feeders, wear a pair of rubber gloves. You don't need to be gloved to fill the feeders, but after cleaning, vigorously wash your gloved hands and cleaning brushes with warm, soapy water. Use paper towels to pat dry, and discard the towels.

Cleaning Your Feeders

Always try to use rubber gloves when cleaning the feeding area because there are several diseases that can be picked up from bird droppings. *Histoplasma capsulatum* is a fungus in soils that is deposited from bird and bat droppings. It is recommended to wear a particulate mask while raking up or blowing away seed hulls underneath feeders. Many people who contract histoplasmosis don't develop symptoms, but some exhibit mild flu-like symptoms. Rarely, other people can suffer serious complications.

Cryptococcosis is another fungal disease found in the environment, and it also comes from bird droppings. Often associated with pigeon droppings, it is best to wear rubber gloves and a mask when cleaning up scat on feeders and around roosting sites, attics, cupolas and other places where large numbers of birds gather. Like histoplasmosis, many people don't suffer any symptoms. Some just come down with symptoms of a mild flu.

West Nile virus is carried by mosquitoes. Finches and other birds contract it but don't transfer it to humans, so there is no need to be concerned about getting this disease from your feeders.

Keeping your feeding station clean and refreshing the site are quick and easy ways to stop the spread of avian disease and other diseases from bird droppings.

A quick dry-clean is recommended each time you refill your feeders. Dump out the old seeds before adding any new and knock out any seed clumps. Also, wipe down the feeder with a dry rag to remove the bird scat before refilling it.

You should wet-clean your feeder if there are obvious signs of mold or mildew. Dead birds near feeders or on them are another indicator that a major wet cleaning is needed. Use a sanitizing solution of one part bleach to nine parts warm water, or purchase a commercial bird feeder cleaning solution.

To remove stuck birdseed, use a scrub brush. Insert a long-handled bottlebrush in tubes, and use an old toothbrush to clean other hard places to reach.

Dismantle the feeder as much as possible and scour with your scrub brushes and cleaning solution. Clean inside and out and rinse well with hot water. Allow the feeder to dry thoroughly overnight or lay the parts out in the sunlight before reassembling and refilling it.

Cleaning around the base of a feeding station is very important. Rake up or blow away old seed hulls on the ground. These will accumulate after a long winter or other extended feeding. Add or refresh any mulch or gravel beneath your feeders.

Finally, remember to wash and rinse birdbaths before refilling them with fresh water.

Protecting Finches

The U.S. Fish and Wildlife Service estimates there are 10 billion resident and migratory birds breeding in North America annually. By the end of the nesting season, there are about 20 billion birds.

The majority of threats to birds are associated with people. Collisions with building windows are one of the biggest killers. Nearly 100 million birds die each year from flying into windows. During migration through cities, they fly into lit skyscrapers at night. Most small songbirds migrate at night and seem to navigate better in darkness. Businesses in tall buildings are starting to douse their lights during migration, and this has helped.

Collisions with windows also occur at residences. The reflection of sky and trees in windows and glass doors creates the illusion that the flight path is clear. This causes tragic window strikes at our homes. To see finches close-up and protect them, move your feeders to within 3–5 feet of window and door glass. This prevents the birds from gaining too much speed on takeoff and reduces impact. Move feeders to least 30 feet away from windows to stop collisions due to reflection.

Apply ultraviolet (UV) light reflective stickers to glass so birds can see objects and not reflections. UV stickers are clear and often bird-shaped. We see through them, but the outside reflects UV light, which only the birds can see. There's also a UV light reflective paint that sprays clear on glass but helps birds see the windows.

Studies show that an effective way to reduce window strikes is to hang ¼-inch-thick metallic streamers from the eaves of your house in front of windows. These streamers block the path of finches in flight. There are many more ways to reduce window strikes, so be sure to check online for more solutions.

Before the bird feeding industry was established, it was common to put table scraps outside for the birds to eat. Very few people would waste any food, so often it was just stale bread or tidbits of other old food. However, feeder birds don't accept morsels of this type, and this kind of feeding usually draws critters, such as skunks and raccoons, that are not welcome in backyards. So whether you set out ground feeders or place food on cut stumps to attract finches, it is not recommended to use table leftovers to feed them.

According to one study, pesticides are responsible for killing an estimated 72 million birds annually. Most pesticide use is agricultural, but you can support the efforts to reduce the chemical ingestion fatalities of birds in several ways. It's easy to help by purchasing only fruit and vegetables grown locally and in season. Buying only organic fruit and vegetables is another option. You may also decide to go organic in your own garden and backyard. Reducing or eliminating your personal use of pesticides and herbicides will not only make the overall environment safer, but the finches you love will be able to eat uncontaminated wild food as they stage near the feeders in your yard.

About the Author

Naturalist, wildlife photographer and writer Stan Tekiela is the originator of the popular nature appreciation book series that includes loons, eagles, bluebirds, owls, hummingbirds, woodpeckers, wolves, bears and deer. For about three decades, Stan has authored more than 120 field guides and wildlife audio CDs for nearly every state in the nation, presenting many species of birds, mammals, reptiles and amphibians, trees, wildflowers and cacti. Holding a Bachelor of Science degree in Natural History from the University of Minnesota and as an active professional naturalist for more than 25 years, Stan studies and photographs wildlife throughout the United States and has received various national and regional awards for his books and photographs. Also a well-known columnist and radio personality, his syndicated column appears in more than 25 newspapers and his wildlife programs are broadcast on a number of Midwest radio stations. Stan can be followed on Facebook and Twitter. He can be contacted via his web page at www.naturesmart.com.